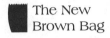 The New
Brown Bag

Taste the Bread

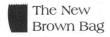 The New
Brown Bag

Taste the Bread
30 Children's Sermons on Communion

Phyllis Vos Wezeman
Anna L. Liechty
Kenneth R. Wezeman

THE
PILGRIM
PRESS
Cleveland

To Rick and Diane Spleth
With whom we share the meal that helps us to remember in the present
what God has done for us in the past and to trust in God to be with us in
the future.

—PHYLLIS VOS WEZEMAN

In memory of Jean Wakeland
Faithful elder in our church. I still listen for his step when communion is
served.

—ANNA L. LIECHTY

To Ann Osterhouse
With whom I have shared bread physically and spiritually.

—KENNETH R. WEZEMAN

The Pilgrim Press, 700 Prospect Avenue East
Cleveland, Ohio 44115-1100
pilgrimpress.com

07 06 05 04 03   5 4 3 2 1

Library of Congress Cataloging-in-Publication Data

Wezeman, Phyllis Vos.
    Taste the bread : Phyllis Vos Wezeman, Anna L. Liechty, Kenneth R. Wezeman.
        p. cm. (The new brown bag)
    Includes bibliographical references.
    ISBN 0-8298-1519-8 (pbk. : alk. paper)
    1. Lord's Supper—Sermons. 2. Children's sermons. 3. Bible—Children's
sermons. 4. Sermons, American. I. Liechty, Anna L. II. Wezeman, Kenneth R.
III. Title. IV. Series.

BV825.3.W49   2003
252'.53–dc22

                                                                    2003055540

Contents

Introduction

For I received from the Lord what I also handed on to you, that the Lord Jesus on the night when he was betrayed took a loaf of bread, and when he had given thanks, he broke it and said, "This is my body that is for you: Do this in remembrance of me." In the same way he took the cup also, after supper, saying, "This cup is the new covenant in my blood. Do this, as often as you drink it, in remembrance of me." For as often as you eat this bread and drink the cup, you proclaim the Lord's death until he comes.

—1 CORINTHIANS 11:34 NRSV

(*See also Mt 26:26–28; Mk 14:22–24; and Lk 22:17–20.*)

Although Christians of various faith traditions have many differences, they also have much in common. One thing that all Christians share is the practice of communion. While our understanding of the holy meal or our way of practicing the ritual may differ from one denomination to another, every Christian church does observe this sacrament. We all share in this sacred rite because of the command of Christ to "do this in remembrance of me."

When we celebrate communion, we have fellowship with our Savior and with one another as members of the body of Christ. The word *communion* is a translation of the Greek word *koinonia*. This term can have many meanings, depending on the context. It can mean to participate or to share in something, to have fellowship with one or more persons, or to be a partner with someone in a business venture. Christians believe that as we participate in the practice of communion, we share in the suffering and death of Jesus and in the promise of his resurrection. Communion unites us with Christ in a very real sense. It also, however, unites us with other believers. This sacrament is, by its very nature, a communal act. It is a celebration of the church, not just of individuals. We may pray or fast in private, but communion is a public act. It is done in private in only the most extreme circumstances. Furthermore, it joins us together with not only those believers in our own location, but also with Christians throughout the world who share our faith in the risen Christ.

Communion is one of the central practices of the Christian faith. It defines who we are and distinguishes us from those who are not followers of Jesus. It is because of this centrality to our life together in Christ that we must take time to share its meaning with those who are learning to take their place in the church. May these messages help children, as well as youth and adults, remember God's gift of salvation every time they partake of the holy meal.

Overview

What is this book?

Taste the Bread: 30 Children's Sermons on Communion is a collection of thirty messages primarily designed for kindergarten through upper-elementary youth. This resource addresses the Sacrament of Communion from a variety of approaches. While each sermon is based on a scripture passage or verse, some lessons focus on biblical stories related to communion, several explain contemporary and traditional hymns used during the sacrament, and others explore theological themes regarding the church's celebration of Christ's institution of the holy meal.

Each message uses a consistent format based on the following components:

PASSAGE: Each sermon is based on a specific scripture text, which is listed for reference.

PURPOSE: Each message's central theme is summarized in one simple statement.

PREPARATION: A suggestion for a teaching tool for each object lesson is provided and, if needed, instructions are outlined.

PRESENTATION: A complete script for an interactive dialogue with the children is offered.

PRAYER: A brief prayer, suitable for repetition by the children, is given as a summary statement of the message.

Although the thirty sermons are listed by title in the contents at the beginning of the book, a significant component of this collection are the resource sections at the end that cross-references all entries by hymn stories, scripture passages, teaching tools, and theological themes.

Since hymns are the basis for much of the message of our faith and are an integral part of worship, they are a logical place to derive ideas for the children's message. Sermons labeled Hymn Stories include suggestion for making or using a teaching tool, a script to be used with the children to convey the story of the hymn, and instructions for leaders so they may prepare for their presentation. Of course, to best connect the lesson with the words of each hymn, an effort should be made to sing the song in worship before the sermon is shared.

Why is this book needed?

This book is a ready-to-use collection of messages to help children explore various aspects of the Sacrament of Communion. Although books of children's sermons might include one meditation on this theme, at most, there is no other resource that puts many explanations of the topic into one book. Since communion is celebrated many times throughout the year, this collection provides a valuable tool for the variety of occasions that focus on the sacrament. Church leaders can readily find help for lessons whether ideas are needed to celebrate the actual communion service, to mark events such as First Communions or World Communion Sunday, or to explore the seasons of the church year.

Who will use this book?

This book will be used in congregations by clergy, Christian educators, Sunday school leaders, and laypersons; in parochial schools by administrators and teachers; and in homes by parents and grandparents.

Messages are designed for children in kindergarten through grade five but are adaptable for boys and girls in preschool and young people in middle grades. They will also be appreciated by adults of all ages and appropriate for intergenerational audiences.

How will this book be most helpful?

In congregations, this collection will be used as children's sermons in worship, homilies in children's church, messages in Sunday school classes, reflections in midweek ministries, meditations in youth groups, and devotions at camp. They will also be useful as lessons in confirmation classes and communion-education programs. In Christian schools, they will be used in chapel services and classroom talks. In families, they will be helpful as a focus for mealtime devotions, faith formation, and bedtime stories.

1

Centered around Communion: Worship's Focus

PASSAGE: 1 Corinthians 11:26

PURPOSE: Centering worship in the Sacrament of Communion, Christians remember the sacrifice of Jesus that unites all believers in the family of God.

PREPARATION: Table (communion table; dollhouse table)

PRESENTATION:

Do you have a table at your house? (*Display dollhouse table.*) Amazing! Everyone has a table? Why do we all need tables in our homes? (*Allow time for speculation.*) We need tables for lots of reasons, but primarily we need a place to sit down to eat, right? Our tables are where we share food when we're hungry to be fed physically and where we find company when we're hungry to be fed emotionally and spiritually.

Have you ever noticed that we have a table at the center of our worship space in God's house? (*Point to or move to the location of the communion table.*) What meal do we serve on that table? Yes, we serve the Sacrament of Holy Communion from that table. What do we remember as we celebrate around that table? (*Encourage the participants to share as much as they know about communion.*) So the communion table reminds us that Jesus gave his life as a sacrifice for our sin. He asked us to remember him as we eat the bread and drink the cup. Saint Paul told the early church that they should continue to eat and drink together in remembrance of Jesus' death until Christ comes again. So Christians all around the world in every denomination continue to share Christ's meal around a table as a way to draw strength and to come together as the family of God.

When we put our communion table at the center of our worship, we say a great deal about what we believe is important in our church. We are saying that the table represents the most significant belief that we share; it is central to our faith. Our belief is that the bread and the juice or wine unite us with Christ and with one another. The table represents Christ's invitation to believers to remember his sacrifice and to receive God's gift of eternal life.

Although many churches place the table at the center of worship, they don't all celebrate communion at the same times. Some denominations offer the sacrament every week. Others share Christ's table once a month; still others may hold communion quarterly or every three months. Communion is usually commemorated on special days such as Maundy Thursday or World Communion Sunday as well.

The important idea is not that churches offer communion in exactly the same way at exactly the same time. What is important is that the table is at the heart of our worship because Jesus' death and resurrection is at the heart of being a Christian. Just like we all need a table at home for meals and activities, we also need a table at church. It's around Christ's table that we find spiritual food to nourish our souls and fellowship to bind us together as a family of faith.

PRAYER:
Dear God, thank you for the table that reminds us of Jesus' sacrifice. Help us to keep his message at the center of our worship and of our lives. Amen.

2
Combined as One: Christian Unity

HYMN STORY: "One Bread, One Body"

PASSAGE: 1 Corinthians 12:12–13

PURPOSE: Achieving unity through the Sacrament of Communion, Christians discover the oneness found in the body of Christ.

PREPARATION: Cluster of grapes, sheaf of wheat; access to the hymn, "One Bread, One Body." Invite the congregation to sing the hymn before sharing the children's sermon.

PRESENTATION:

Tell me, is this one or many? (*Hold up the sheaf of wheat.*) Are these many stalks of wheat or is it one sheaf of wheat? (*Hold up the cluster of grapes.*) Are these many grapes or is it one cluster? It's hard to tell, isn't it? When you look carefully at this sheaf of wheat, it appears to be many separate stalks. Yet it is bound together, and so we say it is one sheaf. Similarly, the grapes look numerous, yet they are still all connected on one branch. So we say it is one cluster. While they appear to be many, each of these symbolic foods is still only one. That is a good reason why wheat and grapes are symbols used in the church. Although we are many individuals, we are bound together through the Holy Spirit as one body of believers, the church of Jesus Christ.

These two symbols also remind us of the meal that connects us as Christians. The grains of wheat can be combined to form one food—bread. The individual grapes can be crushed to create juice or wine. That is why the sheaf of wheat and the cluster of grapes serve as symbols for the church—representing the truth that we share one meal and are one body in Christ.

A favorite communion hymn, called "One Bread, One Body," celebrates this truth. John Foley, a Roman Catholic priest, who was one of four composers known as the St. Louis Jesuits, wrote it in 1978. This hymn follows the metaphor of the body that the apostle Paul used in the New Testament book of 1 Corinthians to describe the church. Even though the body has many parts, it is still one body. These verses also discuss the variety of gifts that people receive, but these gifts all come from one Spirit. In communion, we receive the Spirit of God that binds us together as one church. The Spirit of God is the active presence and power that fills the lives of those who confess their sins and are reconciled to God and to one another. It is through this Spirit that believers are made one as they share in and become the Body of Christ. (*Gesture toward the congregation.*) Are we many, or one?

PRAYER:
Dear God, thank you for the variety of people and gifts you bring to our lives. Help us to allow your Spirit to unite us so that we truly may be one with you. Amen.

3
Connected by Communion: Faith's Harvest

Passage: John 15:4–5

Purpose: Sharing in the Sacrament of Communion unites Christians with Jesus, the true vine, and with other believers to produce a harvest of faith.

Preparation: Bunches of grapes

Presentation:

What do you know about growing grapes? *(Invite sharing.)* Almost everyone knows that grapes come from a vine. Actually, they grow on the branches of the vine and hang down until they ripen and can be harvested to eat or to make into juice, jam, or wine. What would happen if we picked these grapes before they were ripe? Would they be any good? No, they must ripen before we harvest them. What if we cut off the branch the growing grapes were on, would they ripen then? Not if the branch wasn't attached to the vine, right? The vine itself supplies the life to the branch and the branch can then bring forth fruit. Did you know that Jesus used this idea to teach us how important it is to stay united with him? He said, "I am the vine, you are the branches . . . apart from me you can do nothing." We need to stay connected to Jesus if we are going to produce the fruit of faith.

One of the ways we stay connected to Christ is through the Sacrament of Holy Communion. In fact, the cup that represents the blood of Christ is really from the fruit of the grapevine, reminding us of our "true vine." As we drink the cup of juice or wine, we remember that we receive our strength for life from our relationship with Christ. But communion means even more than just our own personal connection to Jesus. The bunch of grapes also represents the truth that our life as a Christian is in community. Just as we are connected to Christ, we are also connected to all others who believe in him.

We are all united by our participation in the act of communion. Not only are believers joined with one another in a church community, but we are also joined with Christians around the world and throughout time. By the sign of bread and juice or wine, we are connected through the ages to those first apostles who passed on to others their experience in the upper room with Jesus. They must have remembered Jesus' message to abide in his love like the branches of the vine in order to produce a harvest of faith. As we drink the fruit of the vine, we remember that we are called to stay united with Christ and with each other in order to produce the fruit of faith to share with the world.

Prayer:
Dear God, thank you for the life that comes to us through our relationship with Jesus. Help us to stay connected to him so that we can share the harvest of faith with the world. Amen.

4
Covenanted with God: Communion's Meaning

PASSAGE: Jeremiah 31:31–37; Hebrews 8:6 (1–13)

PURPOSE: Comparing the Sacrament of Communion with the Old Testament practice of animal sacrifice helps us appreciate the hope found in our new covenant in Christ.

PREPARATION: Stuffed toy lamb

PRESENTATION:

Have you ever heard Jesus called the Lamb of God? Did you ever wonder why we would use that phrase to express what Jesus means to us? (*Children may think it is because lambs are sweet or gentle.*) In order to understand Jesus as the Lamb of God, we first have to understand the Old Covenant between God and God's people. God promised to be the God of those who kept the law, represented by the Ten Commandments. God was faithful; people were not. They broke the law and sinned against God. People who lived in the time before Jesus was born could approach God only through a high priest and an animal sacrifice. The best offering was a perfect lamb, one with no spot or blemish. The high priest at the temple would then sacrifice the animals the people brought to the synagogue. People looked on the blood of the innocent lamb as a way of saying that they were sorry and wanted to be forgiven for their sins. They also believed the blood of the lamb covered their sins before God. In Old Testament times, the animal died for the sins of the people.

In the New Testament, we learn that Jesus came to bring new hope for humankind. Jesus came to bring pardon once and for all for people's sins. The New Covenant in Christ's blood that we celebrate in the Sacrament of Communion is a promise between God and God's people that is not based on keeping the law. Instead our forgiveness and new life are based on our acceptance of Christ's love, which fulfills the law. Because Jesus was the innocent sacrifice for our sins, the Bible calls him the Lamb of God. Rather than offering a perfect lamb to a priest every time we need forgiveness, we can come to God directly believing that the perfect Lamb of God, Jesus, our sinless sacrifice, died on the cross to cover our sins before God.

Communion is our opportunity to accept again that Christ died for us so that we might know that our sins are forgiven. When we share in the bread and the juice or wine, we are saying that we want to live in relationship with Christ. And that is the joy of the New Covenant. Our Lamb of God did die for us, but God raised him up again. We serve a living Savior who loved us enough to die for us. And we serve a mighty God who has the power to give new life. The New Covenant in Christ's blood assures us of more than forgiveness. We receive hope that we can live more faithfully in close communion with God on earth, and we believe that we will live with God forever in heaven.

PRAYER:
Dear God, thank you for sending Jesus to save us from sin. Help us to receive his gift so that we can live in close communion with you forever. Amen.

5
Covered through Communion: Christ's Sacrifice

PASSAGE: Hebrews 13:20–21

PURPOSE: Participating in the Sacrament of Communion means accepting Christ's sacrifice as covering for our sin.

PREPARATION: Garden sprayer, plant with parasite damage

PRESENTATION:

Does anyone know what this sprayer might be used for? (*Show sprayer and listen to all theories.*) Maybe this plant will give you a hint. (*Display plant.*) It appears to have something eating away at its leaves, doesn't it? Now, what might we do with this garden sprayer that would help this poor plant resist the bugs that seem to be destroying it? Ah, we could spray something on the plant to get rid of the insect or disease that is attacking it. However, we must be careful what we spray on living plants. Not everything is good for the plant or good for the environment. But if we care for the health of our plant, then we will search for just the right substance that will protect the leaves without hurting our earth, right?

When we care for our flowers or vegetables, we want to take good care of them so they can grow and produce the beautiful blossoms or delicious food that we enjoy. Do you suppose God feels the same way about us? I think so. Has God provided any special protection or covering to care for you and me? The answer is yes! When we participate in Holy Communion, we remember that the cup represents Jesus' blood. In the book of Hebrews in the Bible, the writer says that through the blood of Jesus we have an eternal covenant, a promise that protects us always. Jesus has covered our sins—removed those things that separate us from God and from others.

The Bible tells us that even while we were sinners Christ died for us. Jesus' sacrifice on the cross, the shedding of his blood, is God's protective covering of forgiveness offered freely to us. When we understand that Christ's loving sacrifice covers us, we want to begin to grow, to become the person we were meant to be. And we can respond in hope because through the power of Christ's blood, sin and death no longer have control over us. Forgiveness is ours.

PRAYER:
Dear God, thank you for the forgiving love that covers us. We respond to you by growing deep roots of faith. Amen.

6
Discovered in Communion: Manna's Meaning

HYMN STORY: "Bread of the World, in Mercy Broken"

PASSAGE: Exodus 16:31–32; John 6:48–51

PURPOSE: Discovering the Sacrament of Communion as God's gift of grace inspires us to freely receive and to freely share the bread of life.

PREPARATION: Family cookbook or recipe; access to the hymn, "Bread of the World, In Mercy Broken." Invite the congregation to sing the hymn before sharing the children's sermon.

PRESENTATION:

At special times, like birthdays or holidays, does your family serve a favorite food based on a handed-down recipe? This cookbook (or recipe card) contains my family's favorite recipes. (Explain the special food and the source of the recipe such as a grandparent or a distant relative.) So whenever our family gathers and shares this special food, it is a time to remember and to celebrate one of the traditions that helps to strengthen our relationships.

In the church we share a special meal that has a long history, too. One of the recipes for that meal can be found in the Old Testament book of Exodus. When Moses was leading the people of Israel out of Egypt, God provided them a special food in the wilderness called *manna*. Manna was a tiny, white substance that covered the ground every morning, just like dew covers the grass. The Israelites could gather what they needed for the day and use the manna to make honey-flavored bread, like pancakes or tortillas. This food was God's gift to them to keep the people alive in the wilderness, where there wasn't a way to grow crops. God told Moses that the Israelites should store some of the manna in their special place of worship so that they would always remember God's mercy that fed them for forty years.

In the New Testament, Jesus reminded his followers of the manna in the desert that fed God's people. And he added another meaning to the idea of manna. Jesus said that his life represented a new manna from heaven that was even better than the Old Testament type. When we eat the bread in communion that represents Jesus' sacrifice of his body for our sins, we receive a manna that gives us eternal life. Just like the manna of the wilderness was God's free gift of love and mercy to the people of Israel, Jesus, our bread of life, is a gift of God's grace that we cannot earn or deserve, only receive with thanksgiving.

Sometimes we may forget what the elements of communion mean to us. One of the best ways to be reminded of their meaning is in the songs we sing to get ready to receive the bread and juice or wine. Reginald Heber, an Anglican Bishop in the early 1800s, wrote many hymns for the church. One that we still sing today is called "Bread of the World, in Mercy Broken." The original title was "Before the Sacrament," because Heber felt that the hymn invited people to confess their sin and accept the grace of God as their souls were fed. Passing along the words of this song is like handing down a family recipe. When we discover the special ingredients of *mercy* and *grace* in our manna called communion, then we strengthen our bonds as the family of God. But more importantly we hand on to future generations the recipe that ensures people can be fed for eternity.

PRAYER:
Dear God, thank you for the manna that you give us each day. Help us to remember to be thankful for your gift of mercy and grace that we find in communion with Christ, our Bread of Life. Amen.

7
Encompassed in Communion: God's People

PASSAGE: 1 Corinthians 10:17

PURPOSE: Acknowledging God's world in the Sacrament of Communion leads us to unity as the people of God.

PREPARATION: Bread representative of each continent, such as chapitas from Africa, marbled bread from Antarctica, rice cakes from Asia, wheat bread from Australia, rye bread from Europe, corn bread from North America, or tortillas from South America.

PRESENTATION:

What is something the whole world shares in common? *(Display a basket containing various types of bread.)* Yes, we all eat bread. *(Hold up each kind of bread and name the continent where it might be eaten.)* We enjoy tasting breads from around the world. And since today is World Communion Sunday, this is a good time to think about the different lands and people this bread represents.

Did you know that today was World Communion Sunday? Many years ago the Presbyterian denomination set aside the first Sunday of October to observe the Sacrament of Communion in every one of its congregations throughout the world. By the 1940s the National Council of Churches of Christ began promoting the idea to its member faith communities to celebrate the body of Christ on every continent. Today the World Council of Churches counts on individual denominations to continue the observance of World Communion in our churches. We are celebrating the sacrament in our congregation today just as most of our sister churches around the world are doing on this Sunday.

This variety of bread serves to remind us that we are all different in many ways. Yet this basket really only contains one food—bread. As Christians, we are also different from one denomination to another, even from one church to another. Yet we all share in common one very important ingredient: our faith in Jesus, God's son, our Savior. World Communion Sunday is a day to celebrate our differences as countries, cultures, and people. But it is also a day to celebrate our unity—we are all Christians, made one in the body of Christ, the church.

PRAYER:
Dear God, thank you for helping us to remember that, even with our differences, we are all one in your love. Amen.

8

Expressed in Communion: Believer's Attitude

PASSAGE: Psalm 116:12–13

PURPOSE: Expressing our faith through the Sacrament of Communion, we prepare our hearts with an attitude of thanksgiving.

PREPARATION: Magnetic letters A, E, F, S, and T; metal tray

PRESENTATION:

Who can read the word I've spelled? (*Hold up a metal tray with the word* FEAST *spelled with magnetic letters.*) Yes, F-E-A-S-T spells FEAST. Who knows what a feast is? (*Allow the participants to share ideas.*) Good! Some of you have participated in feasts, right? A feast is a special celebration with lots of good food, like a family picnic or a Thanksgiving dinner.

Do we have a feast that we sometimes share in worship? Yes, we experience the feast of Christ's table or the Sacrament of Communion. What does that feast celebrate? (*Prompt listeners to respond that Jesus rose from the dead.*) When we remember that Jesus triumphed over sin and death, we can't help but rejoice! And when we remember that Jesus invites the whole world to share in his victory, that's a real celebration. So the Sacrament of Communion is a feast, right?

What happens when I remove the "E" from the word FEAST? (*Remove the letter "E" from the tray.*) Now I have the word FAST. What is a fast? (*Prompt listeners to understand that a fast means doing without food.*) Sometimes people go without food to help them pay special attention to an important day of remembrance or to recall the sacrifice that others have made. Sometimes people fast and go without food in order to concentrate on something even more important than eating, like offering their prayers for the hungry people of the world.

Can the Sacrament of Communion also be a fast? Yes, actually, it can. When we remember the sacrifice that Jesus made, our hearts are sad. The simple bit of bread and the small amount of juice or wine are very little food, but they remind us of the body and the blood of Christ and the high cost of our forgiveness. At those moments, we think of communion more as a fast than as a feast.

So, should we be happy or sad when we come to communion? Is it a feast or a fast? The answer is that it is both! We must not forget to be sorry for our sin, and we must remember the price Jesus paid for our forgiveness. However, Jesus calls us to abundant life. Jesus did not stay dead—he arose. Because Jesus lives, we know that we too shall live. That is really cause for celebration. Our job is to prepare our hearts for communion, knowing when to fast from our selfish attitudes and when to feast at God's table with rejoicing. Only God can prepare a meal that fulfills both of these needs. Only God can turn a fast into a feast. (*Replace the "E" to spell* FEAST.)

PRAYER:
Dear God, thank you for offering the perfect meal to us. Help us to prepare our hearts to fast and to feast at your table. Amen.

9

Filled by Faith: Spiritual Food

PASSAGE: John 6:1–13, 22–59; Ephesians 3:16–17

PURPOSE: Eating the elements of the Sacrament of Communion reminds us that Jesus feeds us spiritually as well as physically.

PREPARATION: Breadbasket

PRESENTATION:

What do we usually put in a basket like this? (*Accept responses.*) Yes, we often place a loaf of bread in a basket before we serve it at a meal. Do you think that the bread in this basket or even two, three, four, or five baskets would feed over five thousand people? (*Most children should answer no.*) We wouldn't think so, right? Well, let me tell you a story about Jesus and maybe you'll change your mind.

When Jesus was on earth, he traveled throughout the Holy Land performing miracles in God's name and sharing stories about God's love. One day, as Jesus was teaching, a large crowd gathered on a hillside near the Sea of Galilee. Jesus realized that these people would soon be hungry, so he asked his disciples what food was available for a meal. Andrew, Simon Peter's brother, remarked that a young boy offered five barley loaves and two fish. With those ingredients Jesus proceeded to feed the crowd of more than five thousand men, women, and children. And, guess what, there were twelve baskets of food left over as well. Because of this miracle, the people wanted to make Christ their leader. But Jesus had other things in mind.

The very next day, according to the Gospel of John (6:22–59), Jesus told his followers that he had more to offer them than the food they had eaten on the hillside. Jesus said that he would provide a different kind of sustenance—spiritual food—his body and his blood. That kind of food, he told them, would nourish their eternal life as well as their physical life. Of course, Jesus was speaking of the sacrifice that he would make for us on the cross when he gave his body and his blood for the forgiveness of our sins. And it is this sacrifice that we remember when we celebrate the Sacrament of Communion. Using the symbols of food and drink, the elements that sustain our physical life, we commemorate the fact that Jesus gave himself so that we can nourish our spiritual selves as well.

When we participate in the holy meal, we should also remember the words of the apostle Paul, who wrote, "I pray that . . . you may be strengthened in your inner being with power through his Spirit, and that Christ may dwell in your hearts through faith" (Eph 3:16–17).

PRAYER:
Dear God, thank you for feeding us spiritually, as well as physically. Thank you for the gift of Jesus who offers us eternal life. Amen.

10
Focused on Remembrance: Communion's Methods

PASSAGE: Psalm 34:8

PURPOSE: Experiencing the Sacrament of Communion unites believers regardless of the chosen method for celebrating God's goodness.

PREPARATION: Potato

PRESENTATION:

What's your favorite way to fix this vegetable? (*Hold up the potato and share or suggest possibilities.*) There are lots of methods for preparing potatoes, aren't there? We can mash them, bake them, fry them, dice them, boil, steam, or rice them, but they are still potatoes. The potato is a very versatile vegetable! We may all have our favorite method of preparation, but the bottom line is that we are still eating the same food.

This humble potato can teach us something about the spiritual food that we share as Christians. The bread and cup that represents our holy meal can be served in many different ways. Some variations occur around the physical properties of the elements themselves. Many churches use whole loaves of bread from which each communicant breaks a piece; other congregations serve bread already cut into individual cubes. Still others offer wafers that are placed into believers' cupped hands or directly onto their tongues. Around the world, local churches use the breads that are common in their areas, maybe brown bread or pita bread, bread that has yeast and has raised, or bread that is unleavened and is flat. Individual cups or a shared cup may contain grape juice or may hold wine.

Not only may the elements themselves differ, but the method of serving them varies too. Sometimes people come forward to receive the bread and juice or wine of communion; often they remain seated in their pews. Many churches have railings where believers kneel, while in other places people might sit in small groups around tables. At times, the bread and juice or wine are held until all have been served so that communicants may partake together; at other times each person eats and drinks as he or she is served, making communion an individual experience. Communion can also be a shared experience with individuals offering the elements to each other. Another method for serving communion is called *intinction*. In this approach, the bread or wafer is dipped in the cup of juice or wine, and both elements of communion are received at the same time. No matter the method of preparing and serving the food for our holy meal, however, the intent is always to respond to Jesus' command to, "Do this in remembrance of me."

PRAYER:
Dear God, thank you for the many methods we have to share around your table. Help us to look for the ways we are united by the simple meal that Jesus shares with us. Amen.

11
Fulfilled in Communion: Passover's Promise

PASSAGE: Exodus 12:13; 1 Corinthians 5:7

PURPOSE: Commemorating the Sacrament of Communion reminds us of the story of Passover, when God saved the Israelites from death.

PREPARATION: Matzah (unleavened bread)

PRESENTATION:
What kind of bread is this? (*Some may say it is a cracker; others may be aware that it is called matzah or unleavened bread.*) This is unleavened bread, called *matzah*. By *unleavened* we mean that it has no yeast in it to make it rise like other kinds of bread. That's why it is flat like a cracker. Matzah is the kind of bread the people of Israel ate when they celebrated the first Passover. If you remember, the story of Passover comes from the book of Exodus, when Moses led the people out of their slavery in Egypt. Egypt's Pharaoh did not want to let the Israelites go back to their land, so God sent ten plagues to try to convince Pharaoh to change his mind. The last plague caused the firstborn male child in each family to die, even Pharaoh's son. But the Israelite's were spared because God told Moses to have them mark the doors of their houses with the blood of a lamb so the angel of death would "pass over." This time Pharaoh agreed to let the Israelites go, so they left in a hurry before Pharaoh might change his mind. In fact, they left so fast that they didn't have time to let the bread rise, so they made unleavened bread and the hot sun baked it on their backs as they fled.

God instituted Passover as a special celebration for the Jewish people so that they would always remember how God saved them from slavery and death. One of the special foods of Passover is matzah, the bread they had to eat as they left Egypt and slavery behind.

Passover was the meal Jesus celebrated with his disciples when he instituted for Christians the Sacrament of Holy Communion. Matzah was the bread Jesus broke and passed to his disciples as he said, "This is my body broken for you." He took the last cup of the Passover meal, the Elijah cup, and told his disciples, "This is the blood of the covenant which is poured out for many for the forgiveness of sin." Just like the blood of the lamb saved the Israelites from slavery and death, Christ's sacrifice for us saves us from slavery to sin and offers us eternal life.

So the story of Passover and the story of Communion are very closely connected. The important idea to remember is that it is God's saving power that protects the people who choose to follow God's ways. The reason to keep Passover and the reason to keep communion are the same: to remember in the present what God has done for us in the past and to trust God to be with us in the future.

PRAYER:
Dear God, thank you for the meal that reminds us of your protection. Help us to remember Christ's sacrifice that saves us from sin and death. Amen.

12
Gathered in Communion: God's World

HYMN STORY: "Sheaves of Summer" ("Una Espiga")

PASSAGE: Galatians 3:26–28

PURPOSE: Gathering in the Sacrament of Communion, we recognize that we are all one in Christ Jesus.

PREPARATION: Rhythm instruments from many countries, such as castanets from Spain, maracas from Mexico, and a thumb piano from Africa; access to the hymn, "Sheaves of Summer" ("Una Espiga.") Invite the congregation to sing the hymn before sharing the children's sermon.

PRESENTATION:

(Hold up maracas and create a Latin rhythm.) This music makes you want to shout, "Ole!" doesn't it? Have you ever played the maracas? These are rhythm instruments that you might expect to hear in Haiti or Mexico or Spain. Although people of every country and culture enjoy music, the music sounds a little different from one place to another. *(If possible, demonstrate a wide variety of rhythm instruments.)* Isn't it wonderful that we can enjoy all different kinds of music? How boring it would be if only one kind of music was allowed!

God designed the church to be like a rhythm band. All over the world Christians sing and play music to praise God and to honor Jesus, their Savior. The music might sound different from one place to the next, but the purpose is the same. On this World Communion Sunday, we remember that Christians everywhere share in common the bread and the juice or wine that remind us of Jesus' gift of himself for our salvation. The bread might be a little different, or the order of worship might seem strange to us, but we are still brothers and sisters around a table that has room for everybody.

A Christian in Spain wrote a hymn that celebrates the ways that Communion draws us together as God's family. In 1973 Caesareo Gabarain, a parish priest, created both the words and the music to the song "Sheaves of Summer" ("Una Espiga") as an expression of our unity at the table of God. It is an affirmation that Christians are "one body" who share "one hope," just as grains join to form one loaf or the juice of grapes unite to form one drink. The song says that God makes us "new people bound by love." On this World Communion Sunday, we should join our different voices and instruments to offer a prayer for God's church—that we may be one! *(If possible, learn the song and play the varied instruments in accompaniment.)*

PRAYER:
Dear God, thank you for making room for everyone at your table. Help us to join in the celebration of your love. Amen.

13
Hidden in Communion: Faith's Mystery

PASSAGE: Ephesians 3:18–19

PURPOSE: Embracing the mystery of the Sacrament of Communion, we accept by faith God's plan to bring us salvation and to equip us for ministry.

PREPARATION: Bumblebee illustration

PRESENTATION:

Have you ever thought of a bumblebee as a symbol for the Christian life? (*Hold up the illustration of a bumblebee.*) There is good reason to connect bumblebees and faith. You see, according to engineers and their understanding of the laws that govern the universe, a bumblebee is not supposed to be able to fly. Bumblebees are too heavy for their incorrectly placed wings to support them. Therefore, because of their design and structure, bumblebees are defying the laws of physics every time they take to the air. How they are able to fly remains a mystery. But the fact is—they do fly.

Every time we participate in the Sacrament of Communion, we are celebrating the mystery of faith. First, we proclaim that although Christ died he rose from the dead, and he will come again to earth to gather the faithful from all generations to live with God forever. We don't know how God raised Jesus from the dead; we don't know how or when Jesus will return. Those are mysteries that we accept by faith.

Communion also celebrates another mystery. We do not understand how simple ingredients like bread and juice or wine can take on special meaning during the sacrament. Yet we know that by sharing these common foods, remembering what Jesus did for us, something uncommon happens in our lives. We know that receiving communion changes us; we just don't know how it happens.

Finally, we can't understand how or why God chooses to use imperfect human beings like us to reveal God's divine purpose for the world. We know that we don't always choose to be the best person we can be. We sin; we make mistakes. Yet God gives the Holy Spirit to dwell within those who open their lives to God's presence. How the perfect Spirit of God can live in the lives of imperfect people remains a mystery, and yet in communion we experience God's forgiveness and renewal. God's grace restores us and reveals God's purpose in and through our lives.

So the bumblebee is a good symbol to remind us of the mysteries of our faith. To those who seek to understand exactly how everything works, faith seems impossible. However, those of us who trust God accept the mystery of faith. Like the bumblebee that flies despite the world's opinion that it isn't possible, Christians celebrate the impossible every time we take communion. Although we may not understand everything, God's love is no mystery to us.

PRAYER:
Dear God, thank you for the gift of faith that opens our lives to the impossible. Help us to know that we can do all things through Christ. Amen.

14

Interpreted in Faith: Communion's Meaning

PASSAGE: Matthew 26:26–28; Mark 14:22–24; Luke 22:17–20

PURPOSE: Interpreting the Sacrament of Communion from various perspectives strengthens the faith of believers in different Christian traditions.

PREPARATION: Photographs or posters of *The Last Supper* by various artists, including Leonardo Di Vinci and Salvador Dali

---

PRESENTATION:

(Hold up a photograph or a poster of Da Vinci's The Last Supper.*)* Have you ever seen this painting? It is a picture of *The Last Supper* by the renowned artist Leonardo Da Vinci. This work is one of the most famous paintings in the world. Most likely, it is the one that many people think of when they picture Jesus' last supper in their minds. *(Hold up another painting of* The Last Supper, *perhaps the one by Salvador Dali.)* Now look at this painting, which was created by a different artist. *(Name the artist, if possible.)* It is quite a contrast, isn't it? Both of these paintings depict the same theme, yet each offers a unique interpretation of the biblical story.

Matthew, Mark, and Luke—three New Testament writers—each share the story of the Last Supper in their Gospels. But even these followers of Jesus interpret it a bit differently in their texts. Each writer stresses a certain part of what Jesus said and did at this important meal, because he was telling the story to a different group of people. One audience may have needed to have more explanation than another, so the interpretation of the same experience varies from book to book.

Just like artists interpret the story of the Last Supper differently in their paintings and the evangelists interpret the account differently in their Gospels, groups of churches, called *denominations*, have different interpretations of what is happening to the bread and the juice or wine as their members celebrate the Last Supper. One group calls it *transubstantion* and says that the bread and wine become the body and blood of Christ. Another family of faith calls their view *consubstantion*. They believe that the bread and the wine are filled with the presence of Christ. Still another branch says that the bread and wine bring about a mystical change within the life of the believers. They call this the "real presence" of Christ. Finally, many Christians believe that the bread and the juice or wine serve as symbolic reminders of Christ's sacrifice. This can be called the "symbolic view." Each of these approaches reflects different interpretations or understandings of what is happening when Christians partake of the same elements. Even with major or minor differences, all of these groups have in common the belief that the Last Supper is important to Christians because Jesus told us to "do this" until he comes again. And, all of these views have something else in common. They all share the story of God's love—the gift of Jesus, the Savior—regardless of how they interpret the ingredients of Christ's meal.

PRAYER:
Dear God, thank you that all Christians share the Last Supper as a way to celebrate the message of God's love—the story of salvation. Amen.

15
Invited to Communion: Our Opportunity

Passage: Revelation 3:20

Purpose: Welcoming us through the Sacrament of Communion, the church invites believers in different ways and at different times to respond to the opportunity of Christ's table.

Preparation: Invitation with R.S.V.P.

Presentation:

Has anyone ever received one of these? *(Display the invitation.)* What does it mean? *(Allow time for discussion of what it means to be invited to a celebration.)* I think it is exciting to get an invitation in the mail, don't you? I wonder if you know what R.S.V.P means; however, I'll give you a hint. It's an abbreviation of the French phrase, *respondez s'il vous plait*, which means "please reply." If someone invites you to a special event, you should always respond with gratitude and let the person know if you are able to attend. That is just good manners.

Does God ever send us an invitation? Well, maybe not exactly with a written invitation through the mail. But Jesus said that he stands at the door of each heart and knocks, inviting us to open our lives to him and to accept him as our personal Savior. Holy Communion is an opportunity to respond to Christ's invitation. By taking the communion elements, we are saying yes and opening our hearts in response to Jesus' invitation.

Not every church extends the invitation in the same way, however. Some communities extend the opportunity for communion to all, some set age limits, or still others require special training or membership in order for participants to come to the Holy Meal. We have many different approaches between and among churches. However, what is important is that we accept the invitation whenever it is offered. When Christ's table is spread before us and the opportunity is presented to us, we have a direct invitation from God with an R.S.V.P.—please respond! We can choose to accept the invitation, and say yes to God.

PRAYER:
Dear God, thank you for your invitation to Christ's table. As we take each element, we are saying, "Yes! We accept your love." Amen.

16
Named by Communion: God's Love

Passage: 1 John 4:9–10

Purpose: Calling the Sacrament of Communion by different names helps Christian's discover many meanings for the sacred ritual.

Preparation: Dictionary

Presentation:

How many names do you have? (*Accept responses.*) Most of us have a first name, a middle name, or two, and a last name. Your first name is called your *given* name because it was given to you when you were born or it was conferred on you when you were baptized. Your middle name may be one that sounded good with your first name, or it could be a name that honors a close friend or a distant relative. Your last name is called your "family" name—the last name of your parents. But besides your first, middle, and last names, you might be called by other terms. Girls could be called "Miss" or "Ms." and boys might be labeled "Master" or even "Mr." Of course, lots of people have nicknames, a shorter version of their first, middle, or last name or an expression that they are called by family and friends. And there are even more names if we count descriptions like daughter or son, brother or sister, cousin or grandchild, niece or nephew, church member or second grader, dog walker or paper carrier, soccer player or spelling champion. That's a lot of names. And each of them helps us learn a little more about you.

One of the sacraments that we celebrate in the church has a lot of names too. Although the ritual that Jesus told us to remember is commonly called *communion*, there are several other terms associated with the act of taking the bread and the juice or wine and recalling that Jesus gave his body and his blood for the forgiveness of our sins. Let's look up the word *communion* in a dictionary and read the definition. We might even discover more terms that mean the same thing. *(Look up the word* communion *in the dictionary.)*

Communion is defined in some dictionaries as, "a Christian rite in which bread and wine are consecrated and received as the body and blood of Jesus or as symbols of them." This term also reminds us of the communion we have with God and with other believers as we share the body and the blood of Christ. Most dictionaries also list other names or words for the Sacrament that Christians celebrate. It is sometimes called the "Last Supper" because it commemorates the last meal that Jesus ate with his disciples shortly before his death. In 1 Corinthians 11:20, the apostle Paul refers to the Last Supper as the "Lord's Supper." So that's another name. One important term for the sacrament is *Eucharist*—a word that means "gratitude" or "thanksgiving." When we use this name, it helps us to remember to thank God for Christ's work for us. The Eucharist is a meal of thanksgiving for Jesus' sacrifice and for God's forgiveness.

That's a lot of names for communion, but there are even more such as agape meal, breaking of bread (Acts 2:46), great feast, heavenly feast, Holy Communion, and Lord's Table. Each name that we use for this sacrament helps us discover a different dimension of what Jesus' sacrifice means to us. Maybe the best term of all would be *love*.

PRAYER:
Dear God, help us to know that we are named as your children each time we take the sacrament that helps us remember Jesus' sacrifice and your love for us. Amen.

17

Nourished by Communion: Faith's Food

PASSAGE: John 6:35

PURPOSE: Receiving the Sacrament of Holy Communion feeds our faith and nurtures our souls so that we may reach out to others in Christ's name.

PREPARATION: Fertilizer; watering can

PRESENTATION:

Does a plant need food and water like you and me? A plant doesn't eat hamburgers or drink milk, right? No, of course not. A plant wants plant food—nitrogen *(display the package of fertilizer)*—and water *(produce the watering can)*. These are both important if the plant is to grow and be healthy, and good gardeners make sure that their plants receive both.

As Christians, how do we get fed and watered? Does God feed and water us? Well, if all creation belongs to God, then it is God we should thank for our daily blessings of enough to eat and drink. And God nurtures us in spiritual ways too—through our families and churches as well as by our prayers and devotions. However, God also provides us with a spiritual meal, a special food and drink that nurtures our spirits and helps us grow as Christians. Does anyone know what special meal I mean? Yes, communion—the bread and the cup that we share to remind us of Jesus' death and resurrection. Jesus told his followers, "I am the bread of life." He also said that those who follow him "will never thirst." What these words mean is that accepting Christ's love will keep us from hungering and thirsting spiritually. We will have everything we need to live and grow as Christians.

What does a plant do when it is fed and watered? Does it just hold all of the nourishment in its roots and feel satisfied? No, a plant grows, doesn't it? It leafs out and reaches out so that others can see that it is alive and well. As Christians, we must do the same. We don't take communion just so that we can feel good inside. We receive the elements of loaf and cup to feed our spirits so that we can grow strong and reach out to others. When we receive Jesus as the Bread of Life, we are able to help others come to find God's nurturing love too.

PRAYER:
Dear God, thank you for providing everything we truly need. Help us to remember that we have plenty to share as we reach out in your name. Amen.

18
Offered in Love: God's Gift

Passage: Luke 2:11

Purpose: Offering ourselves in the Sacrament of Communion, we respond to God's perfect gift of love in Jesus.

Preparation: Manger

Presentation:

Does this look like an offering plate to you? (*Hold up or refer to a manger.*) Well, if we think about the message of Christmas Eve, we might come to see the manger as the container of the perfect offering. God sent Jesus—the only one begotten of God—as our Savior, the one to deliver us from sin and death. What greater gift could anyone be offered? I can't think of any!

What is the appropriate response for such a great gift? What did the shepherds do? (*Encourage or suggest responses that the shepherds came to bow before Jesus and worship him.*) Yes, the shepherds were amazed and excited by the good news and glad tidings they heard. They couldn't wait to tell others what they had seen that delighted them so. What did the Magi do? (*Again, encourage or suggest responses that the Magi brought gifts and worshiped Jesus.*) The Magi were kings themselves, but they bowed before Jesus and offered him treasures because they knew that he was a gift from God.

We have gifts to bring to the altar table tonight as well. Since the beginning of the church, the elements of Holy Communion were used to represent our offerings of thanksgiving to God. Just like the Magi brought gifts to the newborn king, we bring gifts of bread and juice or wine as symbols not only of Jesus' life, but of our own—the fruit of our labors and the treasure from our homes. Through our gifts we are praising God's goodness to us. Maybe it seems a little strange to be celebrating Communion on the night of Jesus' birth, Christmas Eve. After all, it is Easter when we celebrate Christ's death and resurrection. But tonight we remember that Jesus came to earth as one of us. He came to share our experience, our "common lot." He came as God's own son—both human and divine—as God's perfect offering for our imperfect lives.

Christmas Eve is a time for us to worship before the newborn King. As we kneel at the manger tonight, we offer our gifts of material goods. But most of all, we offer our hearts and make room for the Christ Child to be reborn within us.

PRAYER:
Dear God, thank you for offering to us the greatest gift of all—Jesus. Help us to make room in our hearts so that he may be reborn within us. Amen.

19
Prepared for Communion: Our Repentance

PASSAGE: Matthew 4:1–11

PURPOSE: Preparing for the Sacrament of Communion means that we repent and ready our hearts for the gift of God's forgiveness.

PREPARATION: Pruning shears; woody stems or vines, such as grapevines

---

PRESENTATION:

Did you notice all the vines I brought today? *(Display the vines.)* I also brought along this tool. Does anyone know what it is? *(Hold up the pruning shears and invite response.)* They look like very thick scissors, don't they? Sharp pruning shears are a gardener's best friend. But a good gardener doesn't just start hacking away at a plant. There is a best way to cut old growth from plants. In order to keep a vine healthy, the gardener prunes the dead part by slanting the cut away from the bud, like this. *(Demonstrate proper pruning technique.)* Pruning sends a message to the roots of a plant that it is time to start growing again. So pruning a plant properly is an important part of keeping it healthy.

This gardening lesson can help us grow in our faith, too. Do we sometimes forget God and develop problems that need to be pruned away? Of course! All of us need God's help to remove the sin in our lives. Our preparation for communion offers us an opportunity to repent. That means we tell God that we're sorry for the wrongs we've done and ask God to forgive us. When we repent and ask God to take away the sin in our lives, our roots of faith get new energy to help us begin to live in a new way. Like healthy plants pruned by God, we are ready to produce the fruit of faith to share with others. So preparing for communion is an important part of being a follower of Jesus.

Jesus himself taught us the importance of preparation. Before he began his ministry for God, Jesus spent forty days in the wilderness fasting, praying, and seeking God's will for his life. This time of preparation pruned away all temptation for Jesus to misuse God's power. Jesus came out of the desert focused only on God and what God wanted him to do. Each time we participate in communion we invite God to prune everything from our hearts that tempts us away from God's mission.

PRAYER:
Dear God, forgive us for what we have done wrong and for what we have failed to do at all. Help us to deepen our roots of faith so that we may grow to be sturdy, healthy Christians. Amen.

20
Proclaimed in Communion: Faith's Risk

PASSAGE: John 21

PURPOSE: Partaking of the Sacrament of Communion requires us to risk proclaiming Christ's death, celebrating Christ's resurrection, and awaiting Christ's return.

PREPARATION: Budding flower

PRESENTATION:

What word would you use to name this part of the plant? (*Hold up a flower bud.*) Is it a flower? Well, yes and no. Right now it is really a bud. When the bud opens, then we say it is *flowering*. I wonder what would happen if I tried to open this bud myself? Would that work, do you think? Probably not. I would just destroy the blossom. The flower must open from the inside. What if the bud decided that it was safer just to stay inside this nice, tight covering? Then we would never get to see the beautiful flower open or sniff the sweet scent of the bloom. That would be unfortunate. Are God's people sometimes like this flower bud? I think so.

Sometimes people seem afraid to trust their faith. They stay all closed up like this bud, unwilling to risk opening up to the opportunities God provides. One of Jesus' disciples, Peter, behaved like that.

If you remember, when Jesus was condemned to die, Peter denied three times that he even knew Jesus. He was afraid to trust God and to be open to the faith he had learned as he walked by Jesus' side. But God never gives up on us. God won't force us to have faith, just like we know that forcing this bud to open is not a good idea. Instead, after his resurrection, Jesus appeared to Peter and the other disciples and invited them to share breakfast on the shore. They broke bread together, and Jesus asked Peter three times, "Do you love me?" With budding faith, Peter answered three times, "You know that I love you." As he opened up to Jesus, Peter received his mission to build Christ's church. He seemed to be flowering!

When we share in Holy Communion, we are invited to a meal with Jesus. But sometimes, like Peter, we might be hesitant to say that we know Jesus. Are you ever afraid that someone might make fun of you for being a Christian? Or that someone might not be your friend if you say that you want to live for God? If so, your faith might stay closed up like this bud. But just like we are patient with this flower, God is patient with us too. Communion invites us to risk opening up to God. When we partake of Christ's meal we proclaim to the world our belief that Jesus died on the cross, that he rose from the dead, and that he will come again to unite us with God forever. The more we open our hearts to this belief, the more beautiful our lives will become and the more fragrance of love we can share with the world.

PRAYER:
Dear God, thank you for inviting us to share your meal. Help us to be open as we risk living our lives for you. Amen.

21
Raised with Christ: Communion's Message

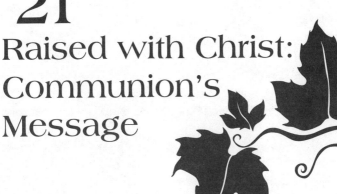

Passage: John 20:1–18

Purpose: Celebrating the Sacrament of Communion connects us with the same source of life-giving energy that raised Jesus from the dead.

Preparation: Live grapevine

Presentation:

Jesus is _____. Can you finish that statement? (*Allow the participants to suggest words to complete the thought; if necessary, suggest "alive" or "risen."*) Right! On Easter Sunday we celebrate the resurrection of Jesus. That means that we rejoice because Jesus is alive! Jesus is risen! I brought a live grapevine to remind us that Jesus lives.

What would you say is the most important part of this plant? (*Let listeners speculate.*) Every part of a plant is essential, but the most important of all is the plant's roots. You see, so long as the roots stay alive, the vines and leaves will regenerate—that means they might disappear, but they will grow back. In fact we could even cut off a branch of this vine and graft it onto the roots of another plant, and it would still live. A graft is a connection made between the stem and the vine that allows the stem to touch the source of the plant's energy and receive life-giving power from the roots. That's pretty amazing, isn't it? We call the plant's power to live again *regeneration*.

We celebrate something similar on Easter Sunday, only we call it *resurrection*. Just like a vine receives new life from the plant's roots, Jesus was raised from the dead by God's power. If we believe that God raised Jesus from the dead, then Jesus is the source of new life for us. That's why on Easter Sunday many churches celebrate the Sacrament of Holy Communion. The message of communion is that through the power of the Holy Spirit we receive the life-giving energy that raised Jesus from the dead. We take in the body, the bread, and blood, the juice or wine, of our risen Savior and that connects us to God's gift of new life, a life forgiven and renewed, ready to be alive to new possibilities and promises.

Through communion we touch our living Savior and our faith is regenerated. Like Mary and the disciples on that first Easter morning, we receive joy and hope. We are ready to tell others that they too can be regenerated. We know that Jesus is alive—and because he lives we too shall live!

PRAYER:
Dear God, thank you for sending Jesus to bring us the power of new life. Help us to celebrate Jesus' resurrection every day. Amen.

22

Recognized in Communion: Jesus' Presence

HYMN STORY: "Be Known to Us in Breaking Bread"

PASSAGE: Luke 24:13–31

PURPOSE: Breaking bread in the Sacrament of Communion, we become believers as Christ's presence is made known to us.

PREPARATION: Portable communion set; access to the hymn, "Be Known to Us in Breaking Bread." Invite the congregation to sing the hymn before sharing the children's sermon.

PRESENTATION:

What is this? (*Hold up a closed portable communion set.*) Maybe if I open the case, you can tell what this is by what is inside. (*Open the set and show the participants the contents.*) Do you recognize these items? Yes, this is a portable communion set used for sharing God's table with people who aren't able to be in church to take the sacrament. Did you realize that people took communion in places other than in church? Wherever believers break bread together in his name, Christ promised that he would be with them.

There is a story in the Bible about this very idea. The events take place on the road to Emmaus after Jesus was resurrected from the dead but before the disciples really understood what had happened. Two of Jesus' followers were headed away from Jerusalem toward a place called Emmaus. As they were walking, a stranger joined them. They were so unhappy about the events of Good Friday and so worried about life without Jesus that they didn't recognize that the person was actually Christ. The stranger talked to them and interpreted scriptures about the Messiah. When they stopped for the night, they begged the stranger to stay and keep talking to them, but first they asked him to bless their evening meal. As he took the bread, broke it, and blessed it, the companions recognized that the stranger was really Jesus. Jesus was made known to them in the breaking of bread. They of course turned around and went back to Jerusalem to tell the others what they had seen.

One communion song that we sing, "Be Known to Us in Breaking Bread," is based on this Bible story of the Emmaus Road. The words, by newspaper editor James Montgomery, were first published in a hymnal, "The Family Table." The words were actually used as a table grace to be sung before a meal. The family table represents God's idea for the church: we all live in relationship with each other, and Jesus is revealed among us when we break bread together.

That's why ministers take communion to people who are home-bound or who are in a hospital or at a nursing home. The act of breaking bread together allows us to feel connected to each other as a family and opens our eyes to see love acted out in Jesus' sacrifice for us. Christ is made known to us too in the breaking of bread, just as he was revealed to the travelers on the road to Emmaus.

PRAYER:
Dear God, help us to recognize Jesus each time we break bread at your table. Amen.

23
Repeated with Reverence: Paul's Advice

PASSAGE: 1 Corinthians 11:17–34

PURPOSE: Following a pattern for celebrating the Sacrament of Communion assures us that Jesus Christ is honored as we participate in the Holy Meal.

PREPARATION: Form for communion service (a book of worship or a hymnal); pattern (for sewing or woodworking project)

PRESENTATION:

Does anyone know what this is called? *(Hold up pattern.)* That's right, it is a pattern. A pattern is a guide for doing or making something, isn't it? If different people use this pattern to make a *(fill in the name of the item)* the results will be the same—well, almost the same. If you follow the pattern, whatever you are making should look just like it is supposed to turn out. A pattern is a helpful guide. After all, if you are making a suit, you don't want to have the legs where the arms are supposed to be, right? It wouldn't fit very well. Or if you are making a toy train, you don't want the wheels on the top when they should be on the bottom.

In the book of 1 Corinthians in the Bible, chapter 11, the apostle Paul gave believers a pattern for celebrating the Sacrament of Communion. Many New Testament Christians were doing it wrong; they were doing it their own way. Some people brought a big dinner to eat at communion, but a few people would devour all of the food and drink all of the wine. Other people who were poor and didn't have much food in the first place would get very little to eat and very little to drink. They would go away hungry and thirsty. "That's not how it's supposed to be," said Paul. "We are all here to share in the Holy Meal. If you don't do it right you dishonor Jesus." So Paul gave us a pattern that we follow yet today. He told us to eat our meals at a different time, not during Communion. The sacrament was different. It was to fill us spiritually, not physically.

While we still follow the apostle Paul's pattern today, over the years congregations have decided how that pattern would be fit into the way they worship. Different groups of churches called *denominations* have written *forms*, or guides, for the minister to use when celebrating the Sacrament of Communion. These forms, found in our book of worship or our hymnal, are a pattern for all of the churches in that denomination to use as their pattern. (*Show the form in the book of worship or hymnal.*) That way, they all celebrate communion in a similar manner. Although there are some differences from congregation to congregation, thanks to what Paul wrote in 1 Corinthians, these rituals are all very similar.

When we follow Paul's pattern, we honor God's gift of Jesus' sacrifice for our sake as we share the bread and drink the juice or wine in remembrance of Christ. And we celebrate the pattern of God's love as we share the story of salvation with others.

PRAYER:
Dear God, help us to celebrate the pattern of your love as we share the story of Jesus with others. Amen.

24
Revealed in Communion: God's Plan

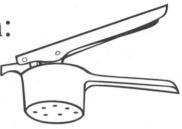

PASSAGE: Matthew 26:36–46, 27:45–54

PURPOSE: Appreciating the Sacrament of Communion teaches us to value Jesus' suffering as God's plan for salvation.

PREPARATION: Food press or ricer, ripe grapes

PRESENTATION:

Aren't these beautiful grapes? (*Hold up bunches of ripe grapes.*) Once grapes are picked from the vine, how long will they keep? Not for long if we're hungry, right? But if we are going to enjoy the fruit of the harvest for more than a few days, the grapes must be preserved in some way. What are some ways to preserve grapes? (*Suggestions may include canning them whole, making jams and jellies, or drying raisins, as well as making juice and wine.*)

In the church, what do we use from the fruit of the vine when we have our communion service? (*Follow your church's tradition by naming juice or wine.*) Yes, in worship we use juice or wine as a part of our celebration called Holy Communion to help us remember Christ's sacrifice. Where does the juice or wine come from? (*Hold up the ripe grapes.*) Yes, from grapes, but how do we get from big beautiful grapes like these to something we can drink? (*Let the participants explain.*) We have to press or squeeze the juice out of the grapes, right? There are lots of ways to do that. One way would be to use a tool like this.

(Hold up the press or ricer. If time permits, demonstrate and allow others to take turns pressing the juice and sampling it.)

Does life press in on us sometimes? Did life press in on Jesus? *(The answer is obviously yes, but wait and let all nod in agreement.)* Yes, during Holy Week we understand that Jesus was pressed by a large crowd on Palm Sunday, wanting him to enter Jerusalem as a conquering hero and throw out the foreigners, the Romans. Later in the week, when he didn't do what they expected or wanted, the crowds pressed to crucify him. In the garden of Gethsemane, Jesus felt the pressure of choosing to accept the suffering of death on a cross. He prayed to God to "let this cup pass from me." Jesus didn't want to suffer in life any more than we do. However, Jesus accepted the pain of the cross if that was the only way to fulfill God's plan to save people from their sins. Jesus offered himself to God saying, "Your will be done."

The pain and suffering of Jesus are hard for us to think about. But we must not forget what Jesus did for us. It is his sacrifice that allows us to know how much God loves us and that provides the way to eternal life. This is why we share the cup of juice or wine during our communion service—to remember Jesus' gift to us of his own life.

Another important idea to remember when we take communion is that all of us will face times of difficulty and suffering, as Jesus did. We will be pressed, just like grapes after the harvest. But what we learn from Holy Week is that if we offer our lives to God, God can use even difficult times as a way to bring good to us and to others. We drink the juice or wine and remember Christ's sacrifice for us. And we remember as well that God can bring good from anything—even from times that seem to crush us.

PRAYER:
Dear God, thank you for sending Jesus to give his life for us. Help us to understand like he did that you can bring good even from situations that seem hopeless. Amen.

25
Satisfied by Communion: Christ's Invitation

HYMN STORY: "You Satisfy the Hungry Heart" ("Gift of Finest Wheat")

PASSAGE: John 10:14–15

PURPOSE: Accepting the opportunity of the Sacrament of Communion satisfies our hunger for God's presence and leads us to service in God's name.

PREPARATION: Shepherd's crook; access to the hymn, "You Satisfy the Hungry Heart" ("Gift of Finest Wheat.") Invite the congregation to sing the hymn before sharing the children's sermon.

PRESENTATION:

What are some symbols that you expect to see when we celebrate the Sacrament of Communion? (*Listen to or prompt with suggestions such as bread, chalice, grapes, and wheat.*) Those are all good examples of communion symbols, but here is another one that you might not have considered. (*Display the shepherd's crook.*) This is a shepherd's crook. You may have seen pictures or statues of Jesus holding something like this. The staff is a tool a shepherd uses to look after the sheep. The crook can help the shepherd lift up a lamb or bring a wandering sheep back to the fold. Jesus called himself "The Good Shepherd." That means that we are his sheep. A good shepherd feeds and cares for the sheep, watches over and protects them, and leads them out to pasture. That is what Jesus does for us as well.

A popular communion hymn celebrates the shepherding love of Jesus that Christians experience as they partake of the sacrament. The text, written by Omer Westendorf in 1976, and the music, composed by his friend, Robert Kreutz, were combined and selected from over two hundred entries as the official hymn for an international conference on the Eucharist, or communion. It was first called "Gift of Finest Wheat," but it later became known by its first line "You Satisfy the Hungry Heart." The first stanza begins with the idea of Jesus as the Good Shepherd, whose sheep hear and know his voice. Other verses remind us that we are fed by our loving shepherd and gathered into one flock, the church. When we hear Christ's invitation and respond, then we are filled with his presence and are ready to go forth and serve, just as our shepherd has served us.

So while we may not think of this shepherd's crook as a symbol of Holy Communion, we can understand now that Christ is our Good Shepherd, who feeds us with the bread of life, the bread that represents his loving gift of himself. Jesus said that the Good Shepherd lays down his life for his sheep, and that is exactly what Jesus did for us.

PRAYER:
Dear God, thank you for sending Jesus to be our Good Shepherd, who satisfies our spirit's hunger. Help us to follow him faithfully and to live like he did in loving service to others. Amen.

26
Symbolized by Sacraments: God's Love

PASSAGE: Matthew 26:26–29

PURPOSE: Observing the Sacrament of Communion assures believers of God's forgiveness and of Jesus' love.

PREPARATION: Stop sign (octagonal shape)

PRESENTATION:

What kind of sign is this? (*Hold up an octagonal-shaped stop sign.*) What does it mean? Yes, anyone who sees this shape on our roads is expected to—stop! That's what a symbol does. With one simple shape, we create a sign, an image that communicates a specific meaning to those who understand it.

God knows about the importance of signs and symbols for human beings. Because we can't easily put our faith into words, God gives the church symbols to offer to people so that we might know that God loves and forgives us. We call these important signs *sacraments*—holy symbols that Jesus gave us to help us recognize God's action in our lives. One sacrament is baptism, when God cleanses us from sin and grants us the Holy Spirit as our guide. Another sacrament is communion, when we understand that Jesus gave his life to save us.

In the church, our symbols for the Sacrament of Communion are bread and juice or wine. On the night that Jesus was betrayed, he observed the Passover meal in the upper room with his disciples. While they were participating in this ritual, Jesus took bread, blessed and broke it, and told his followers that the bread was a symbol of his body, broken for them. Jesus also took a cup of wine and said that it represented his blood, poured out for them. Jesus instructed his followers to share these elements—bread and juice or wine—as a way to remember God's great love for us. In other words, Jesus told his followers to use these common symbols as a way to remember that his death—and resurrection—offers us life, eternal life.

So for the Christian, the symbols of bread and juice or wine are signs of God's loving acceptance found in the Sacrament of Communion. Just like the octagon, those shapes remind us to stop and remember that Jesus commanded us to use an outward—physical—symbol to represent an inner—spiritual—truth.

PRAYER:
Dear God, thank you for giving us ways to recognize your love. Amen.

27
Touched by Communion: Love's Remembrance

Passage: Luke 22:19–20 (14–30)

Purpose: Remembering the Sacrament of Communion also causes us to remember how we are to live as Jesus' disciples.

Preparation: Cup of juice or wine, loaf of bread, string

Presentation:

How do you remember things? (*Hold up index finger with a string tied around it.*) One old idea for remembering something important is to tie a string around your finger. That way you see the string and feel the touch of it, so you are reminded to do what you might otherwise forget. In the church we have a way of remembering something important that's even older than the string idea. (*Hold up or point to the cup of juice or wine and the loaf of bread.*) God understood that we would need a way to recall Jesus' message of love as well as a way to remember how we are to live as Jesus' disciples.

On the last night that Jesus and his disciples celebrated the Passover, Jesus helped them to see God's gift of that meal in a new way. Jesus took bread, blessed and broke it, and shared the bread with them saying, "This is my body which is given for you. Do this in remembrance of me." On that same night, Jesus also took the cup saying, "This cup that is poured out for you is the new covenant in my blood." The loaf and cup become symbols to help us remember that

Jesus gave his life for each one of us. Eating the bread and drinking the juice or wine also remind us that we are called to offer our lives in service to God's people, just as Jesus poured out his life for others.

Although we can read this story in the Bible, experiencing the meal helps us remember its meaning. Communion touches our senses and helps us remember the message that Jesus offered his disciples on that Passover night—I give my life for you. Just think about the ways that this simple meal helps us understand Jesus' message. We can see the bread and cup and know they represent Christ's body and blood. We can hear the bread break and the juice or wine pour and understand that Christ's body was broken and that his life was poured out for us. We can smell, taste, and touch the elements as we take, eat, remember, and believe the message that Christ died and was raised again. Through this meal we experience the forgiveness of our sins and receive the hope of everlasting life in a way we can never forget.

If communion causes us to remember what Jesus did for us, then we will live as Jesus' disciples. Our lives will reflect the message of the loaf of bread and the cup of juice or wine to all of the world: you are loved and forgiven—don't forget! (*Hold up finger with string.*)

PRAYER:
Dear God, thank you for the meal that helps us remember what Jesus did for us. Help us to live so that others will experience Jesus' message of love and forgiveness. Amen.

28
Translated Through Communion: Love's Language

HYMN STORY: "Let Us Talents and Tongues Employ"

PASSAGE: Acts 2:42

PURPOSE: Translating the Sacrament of Communion into the language of love is the responsibility of those who share Christ's meal.

PREPARATION: Greek New Testament; access to the hymn, "Let Us Talents and Tongues Employ." Invite the congregation to sing the hymn before sharing the children's sermon.

PRESENTATION:

How many of you speak Greek? That's not very many people! *(Hold up the Greek New Testament.)* Then I guess you can't help me translate this New Testament from its original language, Greek, into English. In order for us to read the Bible in English, someone had to translate it for us; that means read the text in Greek and then find English words with the same meaning. Translating all of the verses in the New Testament would have been a difficult job!

Languages have kept people from understanding each other for a long time. At Pentecost, people from many nations gathered in Jerusalem for a harvest festival. The upper room, where the followers of Jesus were meeting, was near the marketplace, where these people using different languages congregated to bargain. After receiving the

Holy Spirit, the disciples came into this crowd loudly praising God. The book of Acts records that everyone who listened understood what the disciples said, just as though someone had translated it for them. When Peter addressed the crowd, three thousand people accepted Christ as the Messiah and were baptized as believers. These new converts joined the disciples in devout prayer, in the breaking of bread, and in fellowship. Quite a miracle, wouldn't you say?

When these new followers returned to their own countries, they probably translated two Greek words at the heart of the Christian message: *agape* and *koinonia*. In English, agape can be translated as the word *love*, and koinonia into the word *fellowship*. However, each means more than English can say. In Greek, there are many words for *love*. Agape is unconditional love, a type of love that asks nothing in return. Koinonia, more than fellowship, means the very presence of God, the *shalom* of Hebrew, the peace that descends when two or three are gathered in Christ's name.

As Christians, we still struggle to translate the meaning of God's love and God's presence for ourselves and for others. Jesus translated the meaning of love through the sacrifice of the cross, giving himself completely for our sin. And the Holy Spirit translated the meaning of fellowship, showing that when we are filled with God's Spirit nothing can separate us from God or from one another, not even language. That is why the Sacrament of Communion is sometimes called an Agape Meal or Love Feast, and the fellowship shared with God and with other believers is known as koinonia. Christians around the world use those two Greek words to express the meaning found in sharing Christ's table.

Music is also a universal language used to communicate God's love and God's presence. One contemporary hymn, "Let Us Talents and Tongues Employ," celebrates the truth that Christ calls us to be one people, no matter our language or our heritage. The tune is a Jamaican melody composed by Doreen Potter who gave it to her neighbor, Fred Kaan, asking him to add the words. He decided it should be a celebration hymn for communion and wrote what he called "Communion Calypso." The happy rhythm of this hymn, as well as the words, remind us that we are called to translate God's message of love and fellowship with our very lives. We can only become the translators, however, if we learn to speak God's language.

PRAYER:

Dear God, thank you for sending Jesus to translate your law into love. Help us to experience your love so that we can communicate that language to others. Amen.

29
United in Christ: Believer's Confirmation

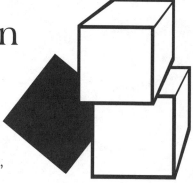

HYMN STORY: "I Come with Joy"

PASSAGE: Ephesians 2:19–22

PURPOSE: Choosing to participate in the Sacrament of Communion confirms our intent to live for God and unites us with other believers.

PREPARATION: Blocks; access to the hymn, "I Come with Joy." Invite the congregation to sing the hymn before sharing the children's sermon.

PRESENTATION:
Will you help me build a church with these blocks? (*Create a simple building with wooden blocks.*) What would happen if I pulled out this block on the corner? Do you think it would (*pull out a block from the bottom corner*) fall? Oops. Yes, I guess so! That must be why the cornerstone of a building is so important. And that must be why we learn in confirmation to call Jesus the cornerstone of the church. Without him, our faith would have nothing to support it; it would fall apart—just like this block building.

Confirmation is a time when we lay the foundation for our life of faith. We choose to say yes to Jesus as the cornerstone of our life. That personal confession of faith is very important. When we choose to become a Christian, we become a strong building block for the church. However, we cannot be a church all by ourselves. We need other people to help us share in a life of faith. These individual blocks can do little by themselves, but joined with others on a firm foundation, they can create an impressive structure.

Confirmation is a time when we join the community of faith. Often, confirmands take communion together as a symbol of their choosing to accept Christ as their personal Savior. However, communion also reminds us that once we accept Christ, we are no longer on our own—we belong to a larger family of God called the church. Every time the church shares in communion, we act out the message that we choose God for ourselves, and we live in relationship with every one else who does so, as well.

One contemporary hymn, "I Come with Joy," celebrates this very idea of the meaning of communion. It was composed by Brian Wren, an English minister and hymn writer, as a summary of a series of sermons on the meaning of communion. The words begin by affirming that we make the choice to serve God as individuals: "I" come with joy. But then the song reminds us that if we choose Christ, "we" become part of a community of love. The last verse ends with "we" go forth, reminding us that we are "together bound" and sent into the world to take Christ's message of love to everyone. Now, that really is building on a firm foundation!

PRAYER:
Dear God, thank you for Jesus, our firm foundation. Help us to join together to share his love with your world. Amen.

30
Welcomed in Faith: Christ's Table

PASSAGE: Philippians 2:9–11

PURPOSE: Taking our place at the Sacrament of Communion joins us with the body of believers at The Greatest Table.

PREPARATION: Book (Michael J. Rosen, *The Greatest Table: A Banquet To Fight Against Hunger* (San Diego, Calif.: Harcourt Brace & Company, 1994); place card(s)

PRESENTATION:

I brought a special piece of paper to show you today. (*Hold up the place card.*) It's called a place card. If you look closely, you can see that my name is written on it. Place cards are usually set on the tables at a birthday party, a formal dinner, or a wedding reception to let the guests know where they are to sit. Place cards might also be used in a classroom or at a meeting to assign seats to the individuals who attend a conference or a lecture. A piece of paper, like this card, lets people know that they have a special place at the table—a reserved seat.

I also brought a book to show you today. (*Hold up the book.*) It's called *The Greatest Table.* In a unique format, the pages expand and a table extends to provide a place and a portion for everyone, everywhere. When we read the story, we discover that the words are a poem of grace and thanksgiving that help us to think about hunger. But guess what? As we turn the pages, the volume becomes a twelve-foot long accordion book banquet. Each page and each leaf of the table opens as children and their families from around the world share a feast as generous in spirit as it is in food. This story reminds us that there is a place, a place card, at the greatest table to feed every person in every nation if everyone shares the resources that God has provided. That's a pretty amazing story, isn't it? Wouldn't it be nice if it came true?

But there is a story about a table that is even more amazing than the one in this book. And there is a table that is even greater than the one on these pages. We really find the story of The Greatest Table in God's word, the Bible. This table, the communion table, is for all Christians who wish to know the presence of Christ and to share in the community of God's people. Scripture tells us that men and women, children and youth, from the east and the west, from the north and the south, are invited to gather around Christ's table. At God's Great Table we break bread and we drink juice or wine as we remember Jesus' sacrifice for us—his body that was broken and his blood that was shed at Calvary. The good news is that there is a place at the communion table for every person in the world who responds to God's invitation to believe that Jesus took his or her place on the cross and to believe that Jesus offered his life so that we may have eternal life. Each person who accepts Jesus as his or her Savior can put a place card at God's Great Table. Along with our names (*name the participants and hand a place card to each person, if desired*) we can add Abena and Abla from Africa, Anna and Arthur from Antartica, Ahladita and Asher from Asia, Adelaide and Archibold from Australia, Edward and Enid from Europe, Night Sky and Noelani from North America, and Sabina and Salvador from South America. Now, that's really an amazing story of an amazing God and an amazing table. And the best part is, it's true.

PRAYER:
Dear God, thank you for offering us a place at Christ's table. Help us to share this story with others so that everyone in the world receives the invitation to feast on your love. Amen.

Communion: Age Group Suggestions

Communion is one of the most significant symbols of church life. Jesus instituted the elements of a simple meal as a way to help us remember him and as a tangible way to demonstrate Christian fellowship. This powerful symbolism is absorbed by each generation as children observe and then participate in this sacrament of the church. Like all helpful symbols, Holy Communion may be experienced and interpreted on a variety of levels. Pastors, educators, and parents must be sensitive to each participant's readiness to learn to understand traditions and symbols. Use the following suggestions to explore the meaning of communion with different age groups. Consider a variety of settings and situations that would allow Christians, young and old, to study, share, and learn about this most important of all meals.

Preschool: Symbols of Communion

✞ Show commonly recognized symbols and discuss their meanings: heart, stop sign, golden arches, or dollar sign.

✞ Discuss symbols that represent Jesus: church, cross, heart, sheep, shepherd.

✞ Display a picture of Jesus and the disciples at the Last Supper and explain that Jesus gave us a meal to help us remember him.

✞ Share grapes and crackers and celebrate the memories of Jesus.

Early Elementary: Bible Stories of Communion

✝ Read a story of Jesus inviting his disciples to share in the Last Supper.

✝ Draw a picture of Jesus sharing the meal with his friends; put yourself in the picture.

✝ Sing a song about communion.

✝ Eat bread and drink grape juice as a snack.

Upper Elementary: Sacrament of Communion

✝ Read John 6:48–51 in several versions of the Bible; compare and discuss meanings.

✝ Look up the word *sacrament* in a Bible dictionary and discuss how the bread and cup become *sacred*; how Jesus commanded us to use an outward, physical symbol to represent an inner, spiritual truth.

✝ Design a symbol for a poster, bulletin cover, or bread cloth.

✝ Read and act out the communion service from the hymnal or book of worship.

Middle School: Names for Communion

✝ Brainstorm, look up, and write definitions for words and terms that relate to communion, like: Agape Meal, Eucharist, Great Feast, Heavenly Feast, Holy Communion, Last Supper, Lord's Supper, Lord's Table.

✝ Make a communion dictionary for study in confirmation classes, Sunday school, or youth group, or to share with the congregation.

✝ Create a collage, word weaving, or altar cloth of terms that represent the Sacrament of Holy Communion.

✝ Bake bread for a communion service.

High School: Methods for Serving Communion

✝ Brainstorm methods of serving communion: coming forward, passing elements in the pews, practicing intinction, kneeling at rails, participating in an agape meal, gathering in groups of twelve around tables, serving others, and visiting shut-ins.

✝ Interview members of the congregation to find out their

favorite or most meaningful communion service.

✢ Collect responses and write a communion devotional with stories and reflections of those interviewed.

✢ Make a memory; hold an outdoor communion service at a favorite youth location using a unique approach for serving communion.

Adult: Interpretations of Communion

✢ Assign groups or individuals to read background information on theological interpretations for communion in religious reference books: transubstantiation (bread and wine become Christ's body and blood), consubstantiation (bread and wine are filled with Christ's presence), real presence (bread and wine bring a mystical change within the life of the believer), and symbolic view (bread and wine serve as symbolic reminders of Christ's sacrifice).

✢ Have each group list primary concepts related to each theory on newsprint or poster board.

✢ Share information by having each group make a report and discuss the specific tradition of your congregation.

✢ Pray for understanding and tolerance within the Body of Christ; consider visiting or talking with other denominations that share a differing view of communion.

Hymn-Story
Cross-References

"Be Known to Us in Breaking Bread"
>> *Recognized in Communion: Jesus' Presence*

"Bread of the World, In Mercy Broken"
>> *Discovered in Communion: Manna's Meaning*

"I Come with Joy"
>> *United in Christ: Believer's Confirmation*

"Let Us Talents and Tongues Employ"
>> *Translated through Communion: Love's Language*

"One Bread, One Body"
>> *Combined as One: Christian Unity*

"Sheaves of Summer" ("Una Espiga")
>> *Gathered in Communion: God's World*

"You Satisfy the Hungry Heart"
("Gift of Finest Wheat")
>> *Satisfied by Communion: Christ's Invitation*

Scripture Cross-References

Old Testament

Exodus 12:13

Fulfilled in Communion: Passover's Promise

Exodus 16:31–32

Discovered in Communion: Manna's Meaning

Psalm 34:8

Focused on Remembrance: Communion's Methods

Psalm 116:12–13

Expressed in Communion: Believer's Attitude

Jeremiah 31:31–37

Covenanted with God: Communion's Message

New Testament

Matthew 4:1–11

Prepared for Communion: Our Repentance

Matthew 26:26–28

Interpreted in Faith: Communion's Meaning

Matthew 26:26–29

Symbolized by Sacraments: God's Love

Matthew 26:36–46

Revealed in Communion: God's Plan

Matthew 27:45–54

Revealed in Communion: God's Plan

Mark 14:22–24

Interpreted in Faith: Communion's Meaning

Luke 2:11

Offered in Love: God's Gift

Luke 22:17–20

Interpreted in Faith: Communion's Meaning

Luke 22:19–20 (14–30)

Touched by Communion: Love's Remembrance

Luke 24:13–31

Recognized in Communion: Jesus' Presence

John 6:1–13, 22–59

Filled by Faith: Spiritual Food

John 6:35

Nourished by Communion: Faith's Food

John 6:48–51

Discovered in Communion: Manna's Meaning

John 10:14–15

Satisfied by Communion: Christ's Invitation

John 15:4–5

Connected by Communion: Faith's Harvest

John 20:1–18

Raised with Christ: Communion's Message

John 21

Proclaimed in Communion: Faith's Risk

Acts 2:42

Translated through Communion: Love's Language

1 Corinthians 5:7

Fulfilled in Communion: Passover's Promise

1 Corinthians 10:17

Encompassed in Communion: God's People

1 Corinthians 11:17–34

Repeated with Reverence: Paul's Advice

1 Corinthians 11:26

Centered around Communion: Worship's Focus

1 Corinthians 12:12–13

Combined as One: Christian Unity

Galatians 3:26–28

Gathered in Communion: God's World

Ephesians 2:19–22

United in Christ: Believer's Confirmation

Ephesians 3:16–17

Filled by Faith: Spiritual Food

Ephesians 3:18–19

Hidden in Communion: Faith's Mystery

Philippians 2:9–11

Welcomed in Faith: Christ's Table

Hebrews 8:6 (1–13)

Covenanted with God: Communion's Meaning

Hebrews 13:20–21

Covered through Communion: Christ's Sacrifice

1 John 4:9–10

Named by Communion: God's Love

Revelation 3:20

Invited to Communion: Our Opportunity

Teaching Tool Cross-References

Blocks *United in Christ: Believer's Confirmation*
Book (Michael J. Rosen, *The Greatest Table: A Banquet to Fight against Hunger* [San Diego, Calif.: Harcourt Brace & Company, 1994])
  Welcomed in Faith: Christ's Table
Bread (loaf) *Touched by Communion: Love's Remembrance*
Breadbasket *Filled by Faith: Spiritual Food*
Bread representative of each continent (e.g., chapitas from Africa, marbled bread from Antarctica, rice cakes from Asia, wheat bread from Australia, rye bread from Europe, cornbread from North America, tortillas from South America).
  Encompassed in Communion: God's People
Budding flower *Proclaimed in Communion: Faith's Risk*
Bumblebee illustration
  Hidden in Communion: Faith's Mystery
Cup of juice or wine
  Touched by Communion: Love's Remembrance
Dictionary *Named by Communion: God's Love*
Family cookbook or recipe
  Discovered in Communion: Manna's Meaning
Fertilizer *Nourished by Communion: Faith's Food*
Food press or ricer *Revealed in Communion: God's Plan*
Form for communion service (a book of worship or a hymnal)
  Repeated with Reverence: Paul's Advice
Garden sprayer *Covered through Communion: Christ's Sacrifice*
Grapes (bunches) *Combined as One: Christian Unity*
  Connected by Communion: Faith's Harvest
Grapes (ripe) *Revealed in Communion: God's Plan*
Grapevine *Raised with Christ: Communion's Message*

Greek New Testament
> *Translated through Communion: Love's Language*

Invitation with R.S.V.P.
> *Invited to Communion: Our Opportunity*

Lamb (stuffed toy)
> *Covenanted with God: Communion's Meaning*

Magnetic letters: A, E, F, S, T
> *Expressed in Communion: Believer's Attitude*

Manger   *Offered in Love: God's Gift*

Matzah (unleavened bread)
> *Fulfilled in Communion: Passover's Promise*

Pattern (sewing or woodworking project)
> *Repeated with Reverence: Paul's Advice*

Photographs or posters of *The Last Supper* (Salvador Dali, Leonardo Di Vinci, or other artists)
> *Interpreted in Faith: Communion's Meaning*

Place card(s)   *Welcomed in Faith: Christ's Table*

Plant (with parasite damage)
> *Covered through Communion: Christ's Sacrifice*

Portable communion set
> *Recognized in Communion: Jesus' Presence*

Potato   *Focused on Remembrance: Communion's Methods*

Pruning shears   *Prepared for Communion: Our Repentance*

Rhythm instruments from many countries
> *Gathered in Communion: God's World*

Sheaf of wheat   *Combined as One: Christian Unity*

Shepherd's crook   *Satisfied by Communion: Christ's Invitation*

Stop sign (octagonal shape)
> *Symbolized by Sacraments: God's Love*

String   *Touched by Communion: Love's Remembrance*

Table (communion table; dollhouse table)
> *Centered around Communion: Worship's Focus*

Watering can   *Nourished by Communion: Faith's Food*

Woody stems or vines (grapevines)
> *Prepared for Communion: Our Repentance*

Theme
Cross-References

Bread (grain; wheat)

Combined as One: Christian Unity

Discovered in Communion: Manna's Meaning

Encompassed in Communion: God's People

Filled by Faith: Spiritual Food

Focused on Remembrance: Communion's Methods

Fulfilled in Communion: Passover's Promise

Interpreted in Faith: Communion's Meaning

Nourished by Communion: Faith's Food

Recognized in Communion: Jesus' Presence

Satisfied by Communion: Christ's Invitation

Symbolized by Sacraments: God's Love

Touched by Communion: Love's Remembrance

Christmas Eve

Offered in Love: God's Gift

Confirmation

Invited to Communion: Our Opportunity

United in Christ: Believer's Confirmation

Connection/Unity

Centered around Communion: Worship's Focus

Combined as One: Christian Unity

Connected by Communion: Faith's Harvest

Encompassed in Communion: God's People

Focused on Remembrance: Communion's Methods

Gathered in Communion: God's World

Repeated with Reverence: Paul's Advice

Resurrected with Christ: Communion's Message

Translated through Communion: Love's Language

United in Christ: Believer's Confirmation

Welcomed in Faith: Christ's Table

Covenant

Covenanted with God: Communion's Meaning

Easter/Resurrection

Hidden in Communion: Faith's Mystery

Raised with Christ: Communion's Message

Recognized in Communion: Jesus' Presence

Emmaus

Recognized in Communion: Jesus' Presence

Faith

Centered around Communion: Worship's Focus

Connected by Communion: Faith's Harvest

Expressed in Communion: Believer's Attitude

Filled by Faith: Spiritual Food

Hidden in Communion: Faith's Mystery

Nourished by Communion: Faith's Food

Proclaimed in Communion: Faith's Risk
United in Christ: Believer's Confirmation

First Communion

Invited to Communion: Our Opportunity

Forgiveness

Covenanted with God: Communion's Message
Covered through Communion: Christ's Sacrifice
Expressed in Communion: Believer's Attitude
Offered in Love: God's Gift
Prepared for Communion: Our Repentance
Symbolized by Sacraments: God's Love

Grace/Mercy

Discovered in Communion: Manna's Meaning

Holy Spirit

Combined as One: Christian Unity
Hidden in Communion: Faith's Mystery
Resurrected with Christ: Communion's Message
Translated through Communion: Love's Language

Holy Week (Maundy Thursday/Good Friday)

Revealed in Communion: God's Plan

Invitation/Opportunity

Expressed in Communion: Believer's Attitude
Invited to Communion: Our Opportunity
Repeated with Reverence: Paul's Advice
Satisfied by Communion: Christ's Invitation

Translated through Communion: Love's Language

Welcomed in Faith: Christ's Table

Jesus' Blood

Covenanted with God: Communion's Meaning

Covered through Communion: Christ's Sacrifice

Symbolized by Sacraments: God's Love

Jesus' Sacrifice

Centered around Communion: Worship's Focus

Covenanted with God: Communion's Meaning

Covered through Communion: Christ's Sacrifice

Expressed in Communion: Believer's Attitude

Filled by Faith: Spiritual Food

Hidden in Communion: Faith's Mystery

Interpreted in Faith: Communion's Meaning

Named by Communion: God's Love

Offered in Love: God's Gift

Recognized in Communion: Jesus' Presence

Revealed in Communion: God's Plan

Satisfied by Communion: Christ's Invitation

Symbolized by Sacraments: God's Love

Touched by Communion: Love's Remembrance

Translated through Communion: Love's Language

Welcomed in Faith: Christ's Table

Juice or wine (cup; grapes; vine)

Combined as One: Christian Unity

Connected by Communion: Faith's Harvest

Covered through Communion: Christ's Sacrifice

Focused on Remembrance: Communion's Methods

Fulfilled in Communion: Passover's Promise
Interpreted in Faith: Communion's Meaning
Nourished by Communion: Faith's Food
Revealed in Communion: God's Plan
Symbolized by Sacraments: God's Love
Touched by Communion: Love's Remembrance

Methods

Centered around Communion: Worship's Focus
Focused on Remembrance: Communion's Methods
Named by Communion: God's Love
Repeated with Reverence: Paul's Advice

Names

Interpreted in Faith: Communion's Meaning
Named by Communion: God's Love

New Life

Raised with Christ: Communion's Message

Nourishment

Centered around Communion: Worship's Focus
Discovered in Communion: Manna's Meaning
Filled by Faith: Spiritual Food
Nourished by Communion: Faith's Food
Welcomed in Faith: Christ's Table

Passover

Fulfilled in Communion: Passover's Promise
Symbolized by Sacraments: God's Love

Pentecost

Translated through Communion: Love's Language

Preparation

Expressed in Communion: Believer's Attitude

Focused on Remembrance: Communion's Methods

Prepared for Communion: Our Repentance

Repeated with Reverence: Paul's Advice

Proclamation

Hidden in Communion: Faith's Mystery

Proclaimed in Communion: Faith's Risk

Remembrance

Centered around Communion: Worship's Focus

Discovered in Communion: Manna's Meaning

Encompassed in Communion: God's People

Focused on Remembrance: Communion's Methods

Fulfilled in Communion: Passover's Promise

Symbolized by Sacraments: God's Love

Touched by Communion: Love's Remembrance

Repentance

Prepared for Communion: Our Repentance

Salvation

Centered around Communion: Worship's Focus

Covenanted with God: Communion's Meaning

Covered through Communion: Christ's Sacrifice

Hidden in Communion: Faith's Mystery

Offered in Love: God's Gift

Revealed in Communion: God's Plan

Symbolized by Sacraments: God's Love

Symbols

Centered around Communion: Worship's Focus

Combined as One: Christian Unity

Discovered in Communion: Manna's Meaning

Filled by Faith: Spiritual Food

Focused on Remembrance: Communion's Methods

Fulfilled in Communion: Passover's Promise

Hidden in Communion: Faith's Mystery

Interpreted in Faith: Communion's Meaning

Satisfied by Communion: Christ's Invitation

Symbolized by Sacraments: God's Love

Touched by Communion: Love's Remembrance

World Communion Sunday

Encompassed in Communion: God's People

Gathered in Communion: God's World

Translated through Communion: Love's Language

Welcomed in Faith: Christ's Table

About the Authors

Phyllis Vos Wezeman

Phyllis Vos Wezeman is president of Active Learning Associates, Inc., and director of Christian Nurture at First Presbyterian Church in South Bend, Indiana. Wezeman has served as adjunct faculty in the education department at Indiana University and the department of theology at the University of Notre Dame. She has taught at the Saint Petersburg (Russia) State University and the Shanghai (China) Teacher's University. Wezeman, who holds a master's in education from Indiana University, is a recipient of three Distinguished Alumna Awards and the Catholic Library Association's Aggioramento Award. Author and coauthor of over nine hundred books and articles, Wezeman and her husband Ken have three children and three grandsons.

Anna L. Liechty

Anna Liechty is a National Board Certified teacher and chair of the English department at Plymouth High School in Indiana. She has also worked as a religious education volunteer, teaching at all levels, directing Sunday morning and youth programming, consulting with congregations about educational ministry, and writing a wide variety of religious-education materials. She serves as vice president of Active Learning Associates, Inc. Liechty lives in Plymouth, Indiana, with her husband Ron, a retired pastor. They have five children and ten grandchildren.

Kenneth R. Wezeman

Kenneth Wezeman holds an M.Div. from Calvin Theological Seminary, Grand Rapids, Michigan, and has served as a chaplain at Ypsilanti State Hospital, Georgia Mental Heath Institute, Appalachian Regional Hospitals in Kentucky, Osteopathic Hospital in Indiana, and St. Joseph Hospital in Indiana, as well as a pastor, counselor, and teacher. Wezeman is currently the business manager and editor of Active Learning Associates, Inc., and the resource coordinator of <rotation.org>, the Web site of the workshop rotation model of Christian education. Coauthor of several books and articles, Wezeman and his wife Phyllis have three children and three grandsons.

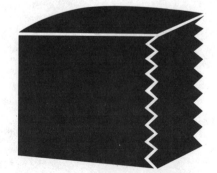